I0748641

The Girl Who Grew Fangs

THE GIRL WHO GREW FANGS

A Book of Remembering After the Fall Into Shadow

DIANA WALLACE

Copyright © 2026 Diana Wallace

The Girl Who Grew Fangs: A Book of Remembering After the Fall Into Shadow

All rights reserved.

No part of this book may be reproduced, stored in a retrieval system, or transmitted in any form or by any means—electronic, mechanical, photocopying, recording, or otherwise—without prior written permission from the author.

This book is a work of creative expression. Names, characters, places, and events are products of the author's imagination or are used fictitiously. Any resemblance to actual events or persons, living or dead, is purely coincidental.

Cover design: Diana Wallace
Interior design: Diana Wallace
Editing and arrangement: Diana Wallace

First Edition, 2026

Printed in the United States of America
ISBN: 979-8-9945774-2-4

DEDICATION

For the one who was told her hunger was a defect,
and her fangs a flaw.

For the one who tried to melt winter
with the heat of her own apology,
only to learn that ice does not listen.

This is for the moment you stopped asking why
and began asking:
What else can I become?

May you discover
that the darkness was never a cage,
but a womb.

CONTENTS

PART II — THE TURNING

PART III — THE INTEGRATION

PROLOGUE

Invitation

Before you begin:
Do not read these pages looking for the girl you used to be.
She is not lost;
she is being forged.

Do not fear the fangs as they arrive.
They are not here to change your heart,
but to protect
its right
to beat.

The winter is long.
The fire is older.

Glow anyway.

OPENING POEM

There was a girl who once swallowed her own sunrise.
She did it out of mercy—
for those who winced at the brightness in her bones.
She dimmed herself into twilight
because the world could not bear a burning.

But light is a living thing.
It claws at the ribs when ignored.
It howls when starved.

And one night—
she cracked.
Not open.
Not closed.
Just... cracked.

And all the unspoken thunder
poured through.

ORIGIN POEM

The Poet Who Forgot Her Name
(ORIGINAL)

She forgot her name
the way a flame forgets it is fire
when smothered too long.

They told her she was too loud—
so she learned to whisper.
They told her she was too needy—
so she learned to starve.
They told her she was too much—
so she learned to shrink.

But shrinking is a slow kind of dying.
And dying is a slow kind of remembering.

For what is a shadow
but a light that has not remembered
it belongs to the sun?

PART I — THE DARKENING

When the Moon Found the Wolf in Her Shadow

Before the vessel cracked,
before the light folded itself inward,
before the dark learned her name,
there was the moon—
the one she became
when remembering first returned to her.

The moon did not make her gentle.
It made her honest.
It stripped the lies from her skin
the way night strips color from a field,
leaving only shape,
only truth,
only what cannot pretend.

Under that cold, unblinking witness,
her shadow lengthened—
stretching past the girl she had been told to be,

toward the shape that had waited patiently
behind her bones.

The old stories say the moon
turns people into monsters.
But the older stories—
the ones whispered in marrow—
say the moon only reveals
what the world demanded be hidden.

And on the night she became her own moon,
her shadow stirred.
A muzzle hinted itself
along the edge of her outline.
A low, ancestral knowing rose
from the place where her fear
had once been stored.

The wolf was not summoned.
It was seen.

This is the instant
the light holds steady,
and what was kept in hiding
steps forward into its own weight.

This is the threshold—
where witness becomes permission,
and the body remembers
it was never meant
to disappear.

The moon did not look away.

The Breaking of the Vessel

She came carrying too much light
for a child
whose hands were still learning
how to hold.

Joy spilled from her
without permission—
a sudden flame
in rooms built for ash.

The grown ones turned.
Not in wonder.
In warning.

The light was seized,
named dangerous,
pressed down
until it screamed.

No law was given.
No reason offered.
Only the blow of silence.

The light had nowhere to go.

So it turned inward.
Compressed.
Heated.

A vessel can only hold
so much sun
before it shatters.

The breaking came
as sound,
as motion,
as darkness tearing its way
into language.

This was the first eruption—
not chosen,

not learned,
but inevitable.

The elders would later call it
wrong.

But the body knew better.

It had saved itself
the only way it could—
by letting the dark
speak
when the light
was no longer allowed
to live.

After the Breaking

After the breaking,
there was no silence.

There was ringing—
the kind that fills the body
after lightning
chooses a tree.

She stood inside herself
like a house
that had lost its walls.

Feeling rushed everywhere at once.
Sound arrived without invitation.
Hands moved before thought.

Nothing made sense
except the need
to keep moving.

The dark did not announce itself.
It gathered—
a low weather
settling over her
until the light
could no longer rise.

It steadied the shaking.
It narrowed the world
to what could be survived
in the next breath.

A new gravity settled.
A smaller sky.
A rule learned without words:

Do not shine first.
Do not open unguarded.
Do not trust the air to hold you.

The body memorized this.
The soul watched.

And somewhere beneath the noise,
the light—
fractured but alive—
waited
inside the rubble,
learning the shape
of patience.

The Pattern

After that,
the body became a corridor
where footsteps echoed
before anyone arrived.

Rooms learned to bruise.
Voices grew barbs.
Silence thickened
like fog that knows
where the cliff is.

Joy rose—
then slowed,
as if passing under a blade
hung low enough
to remember its neck.

The body took notes
the way stone does—
by holding the heat.

It learned the taste
of air before eruption.
The subtle tremor
that tells the ground
to brace itself.

What surrounded her
settled inside her—
pressure without language,
a mountain learning
its fault lines.

Soon the blow
was no longer thunder.
It was weather.

She learned to bare her teeth
the way wolves do—

not from hunger,
but from memory.

This is how pattern forms—
like a scar
that teaches the skin
where to split again.

The dark did not arrive roaring.
It came like a coat
pulled on
by memory alone
when night falls.

Not to conquer.
Not to destroy.

Only to continue
what once
kept her breathing.

Thus the pattern sealed—
a fault line in the body,
a clock buried in bone,
a shadow mistaken,
one day,
for her face.

The Name They Gave the Storm

After a window,

the pattern acquired a name.

They did not call it pressure.

They did not call it inheritance.

They did not call it weather.

They called it *temper*.

They called it *defiance*.

They called it *bad*.

The mountain erupted

and they blamed the mountain

for being made of fire.

Each time the ground split,

a finger pointed.

Each time the heat rose,

a word was placed on her
like a brand.

She listened.
Children always listen
when they are being named.

Soon, the sound of that name
entered her blood.
She began to answer to it
before it was spoken.

This is the cruelest trick of storms:
to convince the sky
it is the lightning.

The body still knew
it was reacting,
not choosing.
But the world prefers
a culprit to a cause.

So the pattern hardened.
Not only in muscle,
but in meaning.

And what began as survival
was mistaken—
by them,
and eventually by her—
for identity.

Appetite (I)

You've changed

is what a cage says

when you've outgrown it.

Wearing the Name

The storm formed—
silence in the air,
Sharp as ice—
before the room decided
she did not belong in it.

Why offer joy
to faces that withdrew their warmth?

Better to bare the teeth
than offer the heart.

She wore the name
the way wolves wear winter—
bristling at first,
then familiar.

If they expected the storm,
she arrived already thundering.
If they feared her teeth,
she showed them
before they could ask.

This is how safety mutates:
not as decision,
but as weather.

The body learned
to move before the silence thickened,
to stiffen joy in its limbs
until brightness passed
for warning.

Better to bare the teeth
than offer the heart.

She rehearsed alertness
the way others rehearsed grace—
listening for the shift in air,

the tightening of faces,
the moment joy became
too loud to survive.

Soon the fur grew thicker.
Soon the cold began to cover
what beat beneath the bone.

And the wolf—
once summoned only in danger—
began to walk beside her
even in daylight.

Not because she loved the dark,
but because the dark
carried what could not be held safely inside her.

What they named her
became climate.
What began as protection
became season.

And somewhere beneath the fur,
beneath the practiced stance,
the light stayed very still—
learning how to survive
inside a body
built for cold.

Inventory

The jaw — where the first No
was swallowed whole at seven
and fossilized into a click
she can still hear
when the room gets too quiet.

The shoulders — where she carried
the weight of being watched
until the muscle forgot
the shape of rest
and held its breath as armor.

The belly — where the girl
still keeps the laughter
that was once too loud,
stored like wine in a cellar no one visits.

The hands — that learned
to pour for others

before they learned
to cup water
for their own mouth.

The feet — that memorized
every exit in every room
before they learned
the floor
could hold them
without trapdoors.

The ribs — where the wolf
curls at night,
the warmth of it
indistinguishable
from her own.

This is the body
she was told
was too much.

She counts it now
the way the living
count gold.

The Cost of Winter

Winter taught her
how to stay alive,
but it did not teach her
how to rest.

Even when the rooms were quiet,
her body listened.
Even when no one watched,
the wolf stayed standing.

Vigilance is a kind of hunger.
It eats slowly,
from the inside.

She slept lightly,
as if the dark might call her name
and expect an answer.
She woke already braced,
already tired

of guarding a peace
that never quite arrived.

The cold did its work well—
too well.

It preserved her.
It hardened what could not freeze.
It kept the heart beating
through nights
that offered no warmth.

The fur grew thicker.
The cold learned how to stay
around what beat beneath the bone.

But nothing meant to save you
is meant to live in you forever.

Fur grows heavy
when it is never shed.

Teeth ache
when they are always bared.

And the wolf—
faithful, unrelenting—
did not know
it was allowed
to lie down.

So she carried winter
long after the storm passed,
mistaking endurance
for safety,
mistaking exhaustion
for strength,
mistaking survival
for a life.

Somewhere beneath the fatigue,
the light stirred—
not yet brave enough to rise,
only asking,

how long

this season

was meant to last.

The Question

It did not arrive as hope.
Hope would have been too loud.

It came as a pause—
a small hesitation
in the long sentence of winter.

One night,
the wolf lifted its head
and listened.

Nothing was wrong.
Nothing was chasing.
Nothing demanded teeth.

The quiet felt unfamiliar,
like warmth remembered
through gloves.

The light did not rise.

It did not argue.

It only wondered—

If I do not hide tonight,

what will happen?

The body tightened at the thought.

Old rules stirred.

Snow shifted in its sleep.

But the question remained,

soft and persistent,

like thaw beneath ice.

Not *Is it safe?*

Not yet.

Only—

Must it always be winter?

The wolf did not answer.

It only waited,

alert but curious,
as if sensing a season
it had not been trained to survive.

And somewhere,
deep beneath fur and bone,
the light held still—
not shining,
not retreating,
just learning
the shape of a question.

The First Rest

It was not sleep.
Sleep would have required trust.

It was simply
not standing.

One evening,
the wolf lowered its weight—
not fully,
not forever,
just enough
to feel the ground
without preparing to flee it.

Nothing happened.

No doors closed.
No faces hardened.

No cold rushed in
to punish the pause.

The body waited
for consequence.
The dark held its breath.

Still—
nothing.

This was unfamiliar safety:
the absence of harm
without the promise of warmth.

The light did not rise.
It stayed low,
watching.

Rest, it learned,
did not always mean exposure.

The wolf remained nearby—
eyes open,

ears tuned—

but no longer blocking the way.

For the first time,

the body touched stillness

without paying for it.

And the season—

long frozen—

shifted,

just enough

to be felt.

The Choice

It was not bravery.
 Bravery still felt too loud.

It was the knowledge
 that she could leave
 and stay anyway.

Warmth waited
 without leaning forward.

The body noticed
 the exit first.
 It always did.

Then after counting the distance,
 after mapping the way back,
 it stepped closer.

Not because it had forgotten winter.
Not because the wolf slept.

But because this time,
nothing closed behind her.

She stayed
with one foot still free,
one breath still held,
testing the space
between safety
and choice.

The warmth did not change her.
It did not ask her
to become softer
than she was ready to be.

It simply remained
what it was.

The wolf watched—
learning something new:
that guarding
does not always mean
standing in front.

Sometimes
it means
standing beside.

And the light—
soft as milk,
golden and slow—
leaned forward,
because the world
did not ask
for its surrender.

PART II — THE TURNING

The Law of the Mirror

The lie was that the cold was a teacher.
The truth is that the cold was simply cold.

We enter this turn
not to find a better
version of the girl,
but to remember
the original form of the Wolf.

It is the moment we stop asking
why the stone does not love the sun
and realize
the sun does not require
the stone's permission
to burn.

Here, the effort ends.
Here, the authority begins.

The Shift

Something had changed.
Not the world—
the story she carried
about herself within it.

For a long time,
she believed the cold
was instruction.

Learned kindness
like a vow taken
against her own nature.

She became so careful,
so good,
so impossible to accuse,
that even hatred
should have lost its reason.

It didn't.

Because the cold
was never answering her effort.
It was never listening.

No amount of perfection
could soften
a heart already set
against her existence.

This was the turning—
not toward light,
but toward truth.

The realization
that she had been shaping herself
around a wound
that did not belong to her.

The wolf lifted its head.
Not in rage.
In recognition.

It had protected her once
by teaching her to harden.
It had tried again
by laying love
where no shelter stood,
offering mercy
to what could not receive it.

Neither failed.

They were responses
to a story
that was never hers to fix.

In this knowing,
something returned
to its rightful place.

Authority
settled back into her body—
not as dominance,
but as clarity.

She did not need
to become better
to be spared.

She needed only
to stop believing
she was the cause.

Appetite (II)

The wolf does not mourn
the den
it can no longer
enter standing.

What the Teeth Remember

The first time she said No
without furnishing it
with a reason,

the room went so quiet
she could hear
her own pulse

learning
to approve of itself.

The Body Remembers Different

The body remembers different now.

Not the bracing —
that old preparation
for the blow that might arrive
disguised as kindness.

But the loosening.

The way a fist uncurls
when it realizes
it's been holding nothing
for years.

The shoulders dropped one morning
without her permission,
as if they'd forgotten
they were built to be armor.

Her jaw ached less.
Not from wisdom —
from rest.

The wolf noticed this first:
how the body began to move
as if it belonged to her,
not to the story
someone else had written
about what she deserved.

The cells themselves seemed confused —
trained so long to metabolize threat,
they didn't recognize
the taste of ordinary air.

But the body is wiser than the mind.
It knows how to unlearn
what never served it.

How to forget, slowly,
the shape of the flinch.

She felt it in her walk,
in the way she entered rooms —
not smaller,
not louder,
just present.

The body remembering
it was allowed
to take up the space
it already occupied.

This was not healing.
Not yet.

This was the body
choosing itself
before the mind
could talk it out of it.

What She Stopped Explaining

She stopped explaining herself
to the air.

Stopped offering footnotes
to her own existence —
the small addendums
that translated her brightness
into something
the cold could comprehend.

For years, she narrated herself
like a foreign film
subtitled for an audience
that wasn't watching anyway.

I know this seems like too much joy,
but let me tell you why it's reasonable...

I understand my voice carries,

here's the backstory that justifies it...

My boundaries might look harsh to you,

but if you knew the history...

Every breath had a preamble.

Every feeling required

a dissertation

on its right to exist.

She exhausted herself

building cases

for a jury

that had already decided.

The wolf grew tired of it too —

watching her waste heat

warming stones

that would never soften.

So she stopped.

Not loudly.
Not with announcement.

She simply let the sentences
end where they naturally fell,
without the apologetic ellipses
that used to trail behind her
like a plea.

The silence afterward
felt enormous at first —
a space she expected
to be filled with judgment,
with questions,
with the demand for more.

But the space stayed empty.

And in that emptiness,
she realized:
no one had been listening
to the explanations anyway.

They'd already decided
what they thought,
and her words were only
ever performed
for her own reassurance
that she had tried.

The wolf settled beside her,
its breath steady,
as if to say:

They never needed to understand.
You only needed to know.

Now when she speaks,
she speaks.
When she's silent,
she's silent.

No translation offered.
No defense prepared.

Just the truth
standing in its own right —
naked of apology,
clean of context,
owing nothing
to anyone's comfort
but her own.

What the Wolf Knows

She learned it
the way animals do—
not by being told,
but by what remained
after the moment passed.

The body listened
for what stayed warm
and what left her
colder than before.

The wolf knew this measure.
It had always known
which steps belonged
to kin
and which carried
the echo of hunger.

Not every clearing
was a place to rest.
Not every fire
meant shelter.

Some warmth arrived
already taking.
Some voices leaned
before they were known.

She did not call this danger.
She called it information.

The seasons,
now distinct,
began to instruct her
without words—
when to open the chest
to the air,
and when to keep
the heat gathered
close to the bone.

She learned
that openness
was not the same
as access.

That what was sacred
could be visible
without being touched.

The wolf did not bare its teeth.
It simply chose
where to lie down.

This was not withdrawal.
This was selection.

For the first time,
she did not confuse
being needed
with being chosen.

And the land itself
seemed to agree—
paths clarifying,
distances arranging themselves,
as if the world
had been waiting
for her to notice
the difference.

When Another Approaches

She knew it
by the way the air remained
where it was—
no tightening of weather
inside her chest,
no inward gathering
to prepare for harm.

The breath stayed low,
as it does
when the ground is certain.

The wolf lifted its head,
not to warn,
but to read
what kind of presence
had entered the clearing.

This one did not cross
before being met.
Did not reach
for what had not been offered.
Did not mistake
her light
for an open field.

They stood
at the distance
the season allowed—
close enough
for warmth to be shared,
far enough
that nothing was taken
by force.

That mattered.

Warmth moved between them
like fire held
at the proper edge—

bright,
contained,
without scorch.

Silence kept its blade sheathed.
Nothing asked
to be tended.

She spoke
and her words returned to her
whole.

She listened
without folding herself
into absence.

The wolf remained—
still,
attentive—
no longer bargaining
for her right
to remain.

When the moment loosened
and the other passed on,
she was intact—
no fur missing,
no scent scattered
in apology.

She did not name this trust.
That word belongs
to promises made
before proof.

She named it recognition—
the ancient knowing
by which creatures tell
what may draw near
without rearranging
the shape
of what they are.

Where the Line Holds

She did not bare her teeth.
She did not bow her throat.

The boundary appeared
the way frost does—
overnight,
without announcement,
because the season had changed.

The wolf stood still.
Not guarding.
Measuring.

Some ground was hers
to keep warm.
Some paths were not
meant to cross her scent.

She did not argue the line.
Did not circle it
with explanation.

The earth already knew
where to hold.

Those who understood
felt it in their step
and slowed.

Those who did not
never saw it—
only felt the sudden
absence of welcome.

Nothing was taken from her
by holding the ground.
Nothing had to be proven
for it to remain hers.

The wolf rested its weight
into the cold soil,
trusting what had been marked
would endure
without noise,
without pursuit.

This was not hardness.
This was season.

And the world adjusted itself—
quietly—
learning where she stood
by where it could no longer pass.

Under a Sky That Does Not Hurry

That night,
the sky did not respond
to her questions.

The stars kept their distance.
The moon did not explain
its absence.

Nothing in the dark
rushed to reassure her
that she belonged.

And yet—
the ground did not release her.

The wolf lifted its head
and looked upward,
not searching for signs,
but noting

what continued
without regard
for her fear.

The constellations
held their shapes.
The dark moved
as it always had.

No message was sent.
No omen arranged itself
into meaning.

Still, the body remained.

Breath stayed low.
The heart did not close.

She understood then—
belonging was not granted
by the sky.

It was assumed.

The cosmos did not require
her vigilance.
It did not ask
for her hope.

It simply kept going,
making room
by refusing
to stop.

The wolf lay down
beneath that unanswering vastness,
trusting the oldest law
there is—

that what holds its course
does not need
to be convinced.

And she slept
under a sky

that did not hurry her

toward proof.

The Distance She Keeps

This time,
the space was chosen.

Not because warmth had failed,
not because danger appeared,
but because she knew
how far her breath could travel
without leaving her body.

The wolf did not hesitate.
It marked the ground
and stepped back—
not in retreat,
but in alignment
with the season that was hers.

Nothing followed her pause
with accusation.
Nothing interpreted
the distance
as rejection.

What was real
remained where it was,
unoffended,
untouched by the space
she kept intact.

She did not watch
to see if it would fade.
She did not wait
for the distance
to become a test.

It did not.

The sky held its pattern.
The warmth kept its shape.

The world did not shrink
because she stood
where she stood.

This was not restraint.
This was authorship.

The wolf rested beside her,
no longer measuring threat,
but honoring choice—
the ancient right
to decide
how near is near enough.

And in that choosing,
nothing essential was lost.

What stayed
proved it was not kept
by proximity,
but by truth
that does not require

collapse

to remain.

What She Carries Forward

She did not gather herself
before leaving.

Nothing needed to be secured.
Nothing reviewed
for mistakes.

The ground did not loosen
when she stepped away from it.
It remained—
doing what ground does
without memory
of her weight.

At the edge of the path,
the wolf paused.

Not to warn her.
 Not to follow.

It lowered its head once,
 as if returning something
 that no longer needed
 to be held.

She felt it settle
 into her stride—
 not as protection,
 but as measure.

The knowledge
 of when to stop.
 The ease
 of when not to.

The seasons did not confer.
 They passed
 as seasons do,

obedient only
to themselves.

She moved among them
without asking
what they meant.

What she carried forward
was not vigilance,
not restraint,
not readiness.

It was orientation—
the quiet certainty
that she knew
where she was,
and could leave it
without losing herself.

Nothing followed her
to ensure success.

Nothing waited
to test her resolve.

What mattered
was not preserved
by her staying.

And so she went on—
not watched,
not defended,
not announced—

carrying only
what had proven
it could remain
without her looking back.

Where She Stands

She did not arrive somewhere new.
She simply noticed
where she was.

The ground beneath her
was neither frozen
nor soft—
it held.

Winter stood behind her,
no longer numbing her skin.
The wolf remained nearby,
no longer standing between her and the world.

The fur still warmed her skin.
The fangs still knew how to snarl.

She knew how to bite.
She knew how to howl.

But what once kept her alive
no longer had to decide
how she was worn.

The light rested
where it could be seen
without being summoned.

Nothing demanded proof.
Nothing asked for a vow.

She knew the exits.
She knew the warmth.
She knew the dark.

And for the first time,
knowledge did not require
constant motion.

This was not arrival.
This was orientation—
the understanding
of how far she had come
without needing to mark it
as victory.

She stood
with seasons around her
instead of inside her.

PART III — THE INTEGRATION

The Law of Integration

The wild is only a danger
to those who still believe
they can be divided.

Integration is the end of the long war—
the moment silk remembers
it is braided with tooth,
and the tooth remembers
it is softened by prayer.

We no longer choose
between the girl and the beast.
We become the one
who can hold both
and remain.

Here, the fangs do not hunt for blood.
They hunt for the edge
that keeps the heart intact,

the line that allows love

to stay open

without being consumed.

Teeth and Starlight

The wolf and the girl
no longer trade shifts.

The sentinel does not wait for the night
to stand between the heart
and the cold.

They have become a braid—
teeth and starlight,
fur and silk,
the wild and the witnessed
moving as a single,
unbroken breath.

She learned that the fang
is the highest form of love.

It is the No
that keeps the Yes holy.

It is the edge of the garden
where the lilies are allowed to bloom
without being trampled
by feet that do not know
their own weight.

She does not bite to consume.
She bites to define the sacred.

The wolf now lies by the hearth,
not because the world is safe,
but because the woman is sovereign.

The fangs are not a threat—
they are the gatekeepers
of a peace
she no longer has to beg for.

She has stopped asking the winter
for permission to be warm.

She simply strikes the flint
against the bone
and watches the sunrise
she finally dared
to let go.

The Disciplined Bite

There is a snap that comes from a cornered heart—
sharp and frantic,
salted with fear and flight.

That was the girl in the dark,
biting the hand
because she feared the leash.

But this—
this is the quiet click of a gate.

It does not require a snarl.
It does not call thunder
to prove its strength.

It is the fang used as a compass,
pointing to the line
where your storm ends
and my peace begins.

She has learned
that to be *good*
is not to be toothless.

To be good
is to be dangerous enough
to keep the sanctuary still.

She can hold a child
with the same hands
that know how to tear a lie
into ribbons.

She can kiss the brow of the beloved
while the wolf keeps watch.

This is the discipline:
the fangs do not lead.

The heart leads.

The fangs simply ensure
that when the heart says Yes,

it is a choice—

and not a ransom.

Correction

They called it healing
when she went soft again.

They called it relapse
when she didn't.

The Yes With Teeth

For a long time, her *Yes* was a debt—
a hollowed-out promise whispered
to keep the room from shaking.

It was a white flag
sewn from the silk of her own skin,
offered before the battle
could even be named.

It was the sound of a girl
trying to disappear
into the shape of someone else's peace.

But the wolf changed the currency.

Now, when she says *Yes*,
it carries the weight of mountain roots.
It is no longer a ransom—
it is a gift.

It is a *Yes* that stands
because the fangs are visible
in the doorway.

It is a *Yes* that is tender
because it is no longer afraid
of being eaten.

It is a *Yes* that is expensive—
not because it costs her herself,
but because it is the only one she has,
and she does not spend it on ghosts.

She can lean into the touch.
She can open the palm of her hand.
She can pour the wine
until the cup groans,
knowing that if she needs to leave,
the path is already hers.

This is the beauty
of the integrated heart:

because she knows how to snarl,
she can finally afford
to be kind.

Her *Yes* is no longer a cage.
It is the sunrise
she finally allowed herself
to keep.

The House She Built

The body is no longer a corridor
where footsteps echo
before the guest arrives.

The walls have stopped holding their breath.
The floorboards have forgotten
how to brace for the blow.

She has taken the wood of the old cages
and built a table.
She has taken the iron of the old chains
and forged a hearth.

In the center of the room,
there is a window that stays open
to the winter,
because she no longer fears the cold—
she is the fire.

The Girl has a bed now,
quilted with the softest parts of the sunrise,
where she can sleep without one eye open,
dreaming of things that do not require
her disappearance.

The Wolf has a rug by the fire,
guarding the threshold
not out of panic,
but out of purpose.

There are no hidden cupboards here.
No hollow spaces in the floor
to stash the joy
she once thought was stolen.

The abundance is out in the open,
resting on the counter
like ripening fruit—
dark, heavy, and hers.

This is the house she built:
a house that is not a fortress,
but a destination.

A place where the silence
is finally allowed
to be just silence.

The Wolf at the Hearth

The wolf did not leave when the house was built.
She did not vanish back into the pines
once the door was bolted
and the lamps were lit.

She followed the scent of the woodsmoke
and the sound of the girl's laughter,
curling her weight into the center
of the room she once guarded
from the outside.

She is no longer a sentinel of the frost.
Her fur no longer holds
the rime of the long winter.

She has traded
the sharp, thin air of the hunt
for the deep, gold rhythm of the rug.

This is the mastery
of the predator at peace.

She does not sleep
because she is tired of the fight;
she sleeps
because the fight
is no longer the point.

She trusts the woman's hands
to tend the fire.
She trusts the girl's feet
to dance without breaking.

Her ears still twitch
at the shift of the wind.
Her fangs still know
the weight of the bone.

But the tension has left the muscle,
replaced by the gravity
of belonging.

The wolf at the hearth
is the heaviest light in the house—
the living proof
that what saved you
does not have to stay wild
to stay strong.

It simply needs a home
where it is finally allowed
to be warm.

Feeding the Guest

She has stopped leaving the door ajar
for every passing wind that carries a name.

The table is set for many,
but the threshold is guarded
by a memory that no longer sleeps.

She invites the hungry,
but she no longer offers her own ribs
as the main course.

She offers the soup, the bread, the fig—
the plenty she gathered
while the world thought
she was starving.

The fangs are the silent guest
at the table.

They do not snarl at the bread,
but they watch the hands that reach.

They measure the weight of the words offered—
distinguishing the kin
who bring wood for the fire
from the ghosts who only come
to warm themselves
by a flame they did not build.

This is the mastery of the host:
to be open
is not to be unmapped.

She can be generous
because she is no longer afraid
of the guest who stays too long,
or the shadow
that tries to pocket the silverware.

If the air tightens,
if the warmth begins

to feel like a debt,
the wolf lifts her head.

And without a single word,
the guest remembers
that they are standing
in a sanctuary
that knows how to defend
its own peace.

She feeds the world
from the ladle,
but she keeps the fangs
for the fence.

The Unbroken Voice

She no longer practices
the silence that tastes like ash.

The words do not need
to be rounded
to fit the narrow expectations
of a room built for compliance.

Her voice has found its bone.

It is a sound
that begins in the gut,
where the wolf's growl
and the girl's song
have learned
the same melody.

It is the unspoken thunder
no longer tearing the vessel,

but moving through it
like a river
that knows its own banks.

When she speaks,
she does not check the faces
to see if she is too loud.

She does not sand the edges
of her truth
to keep the air from bruising.

The fangs have given her
back her throat.

Because she can defend the word,
she is no longer afraid
to say it.

Because she can hold her ground,
she can let the air
carry her fire

without fearing
it will be stolen
or stamped out.

This is the unbroken voice:

a roar that knows
how to be a lullaby.

a whisper that carries
the weight
of the mountain's fire.

a song that belongs to her
because she finally remembered
her own name.

The Privacy of the Sunrise

She has stopped offering her light
as a torch
for those who refuse
to build their own fire.

She no longer feels the need
to burn herself down
just to prove
she is made of sun.

The sunrise she once swallowed
out of mercy
has been released—
but it does not flood the world.

It stays gathered in the ribs,
a warm, gold secret
between the woman
and the girl.

She has learned
the power of the veil.

The fangs are not only for the bite;
they are the gatekeepers
of her mystery.

They ensure
that her brightness
is no longer a spectacle
for the curious,
but a sanctuary
for the invited.

She can walk through the room
and keep her weather
to herself.

She can glow
without giving it all away.

This is the mastery of the light:

to know that being seen
is not the same
as being known.

To keep a part of the dawn
locked behind a door
of her own choosing—
not out of fear,
but out of the holy right
to belong
only to herself.

The sunrise
is no longer a burden
to be hidden.

It is a wealth
to be whispered
only to those
who know how
to honor
the sun.

Tending the Fire

The fire does not stay lit
by memory alone.

It does not burn
because the girl returned
or because the wolf
finally lay down.

It burns because the woman
carries the wood.

Every morning,
she clears the ash
of yesterday's apologies—
the small, gray remains
of the times she almost shrank
to fit a room.

She does not mourn the debris.
She simply makes space
for the new flame.

This is the discipline
of the hearth.

She feeds the embers
with the truth
of her own hunger,
watching the smoke rise—
unapologetic and gold.

The fangs are her tools here—
not for the hunt,
but for the harvest.

They split the kindling
of old stories,
breaking the bones
of forgetfulness
into heat.

The world outside
remains winter.

The wind still tests the glass.
The shadows still lean
against the door.

But she is no longer
waiting for the thaw.

She is the climate.

By the steady work
of her hands,
the house stays warm.

The girl sleeps.
The wolf rests.

And the fire grows—
not a bonfire
to blind the world,
but a light

that ensures

she will never be cold

again.

Wednesday

At 2 p.m., the old heat
rose for no reason —
a voice carried
a tone it didn't mean,
and the mind
split in two:
one half reaching
for the fire,
the other half whispering
I choose peace,
I choose peace,
I choose peace.

And the body
— that faithful,
overtrained soldier —
trembled between them

before the sentence
finished landing.

Nothing was wrong.
It was just a voice.
Just an ordinary afternoon
where the past
and the present
sat in the same room
and disagreed.

She stayed in the room.
She softened her voice.
She let the moment
pass through her
the way weather passes
through an open window —
without closing it.

And later,
when the house was quiet,
she sat on the kitchen floor

and pressed her back
against the cabinet
until the wood
reminded her spine
what walls are for
when they are not
closing in.

What the Fangs Took

She will not tell you about the one
who reached for her
in the old way —
palm open,
voice careful,
the posture of someone
who had earned the right
to enter without knocking.

The fangs did not distinguish.

The snarl came
before the body could sort
this one from *that one,*
before the wolf remembered
that not every hand
carries a leash.

He stepped back.
Not hurt. Not angry.
Just recalibrated.

And in the space between them,
a silence grew
that was not peace,
that was not winter,
that was only
the sound of a woman
learning that protection
has a price
she did not advertise.

Some nights,
she traces the outline
of that distance
and wonders
how he stayed
when the steel
could not tell

the difference

between a lock

and a hand.

She does not

take the fangs back.

But she learns

to open the jaw

for the one

who never

stopped knocking.

When the Wolf Laughs

The weight has finally left the jaw.
The fangs, once heavy
with the salt of survival,
now gleam
in the light
of a different moon.

She has learned
that a snarl
can turn into a grin
when the air
is no longer a threat.

There is a sound
that only comes
when the sentinel
is allowed to play.

It is the laugh of the wolf—
a wild, deep-throated music
that does not ask permission
to take up space.

It is the girl's delight
running through
the predator's chest,
turning the unspoken thunder
into a choir
of teeth.

She rolls in the grass
of her own making.

She chases the shadows
she once thought
were monsters,
finding they are nothing
but the ghosts
of a winter
she has already outlived.

This is the highest form
of mastery:

to be dangerous enough
to be safe,
and safe enough
to be light.

The fangs do not frighten
the girl anymore.

They make her feel brave.
They make her feel fast.
They make her feel
like she can bite the moon
and swallow the stars
just because
she loves
the taste.

The wolf grins,
ruby-stained

with the fig
of her own freedom.

And the woman laughs with her—
because the long night is over,
and the wildness
is finally
fun.

PART IV — THE RETURN

What Is Passed On

It is not the wound that travels,
but the way the bone
learned
to knit itself whole.

The legacy is not the winter we survived,
but the fire
we carried out of the woods
until the fire
became the home.

We return to the beginning
not to remain,
but to show the shadows
they no longer have a name.

The fortress stands empty
because the woman

is now

the map.

The Un-Bolted Gate

She has reached the place
where the bolt
is no longer the source
of her safety.

For years,
she lived by the rules
of the locked door—
measuring her peace
by the thickness of the wood
and the height of the stone.

She thought the fangs
were only for the wall.

But now,
the wolf is knit into the breath,
the woman steady
in her own light,

and the gate
is left swinging wide.

Nothing born of winter
has the lungs
to cross this threshold.

The hatred can stand
at the edge of the land
and stare.
It can whisper
the old names
into the wind.

But it cannot enter.
The air here
is too clear.

She sits on the porch
and watches the evening arrive—
unguarded,
unafraid,

and finally,

alone.

The Climate

The hatred did not move.
The wall of it remained—
fixed,
obsessive,
a monument to a winter
that refused to end.

She stopped trying
to melt the stone.
She stopped explaining
the sunrise
to a heart
that preferred the frost.

Instead,
she changed the air.

The fangs became
the perimeter.

The warmth
the core.

She grew a heat
so dense
the ice could not draw close
enough
to name itself.

This is a legacy:
not the destruction of the cold,
but the refusal
to be governed
by its temperature.

She is no longer
the girl in the storm.
She is the hearth
that makes the storm
irrelevant.

What She Said

The one who stayed called it walls.

Walls, she said,
like something built
to keep love out
instead of something grown
to keep the self
from spilling
into every open hand.

You used to be warmer,
he said,
and the sentence landed
the way a stone
knows the surface
of a lake —
familiar,
accurate,

sinking
before it can be held.

She sat with the word *warmer*
the way you sit
with a photograph
of a house
you can never
explain
to anyone
who wasn't inside it.

hfI was not warm,
she said.
I was burning.
You just liked
the light.

The room held its breath.
The distance between them
flickered

like a flame
deciding whether to stay.

He did not leave.
She did not explain.

They sat in the silence
until the silence
softened
into something
neither had to name.

And the warmth came back —
not the old burning,
but the kind that stays
because it was chosen
by both.

Wide Light

She has stopped looking for the edges
of the room she was told to stay in.

The fangs did their work;
they held the line until the line
was no longer needed.

The wolf does not run
because it is afraid of the dark.
It runs because it has remembered
the length of its own legs.

It runs because the forest
is no longer a place to hide,
but a place to belong.

And she knows—
the unmovable hatred

was only a fence
in a very small yard.

She has already
leaped over it.

There is no more measured distance.
There is only the horizon,
and the steady, rhythmic strength
of a heart
that has finally
matched the speed
of its own wildness.

She is not leaving herself.
She is finally
occupying
the whole map.

The Ancestor in the Mirror

She no longer looks into the glass
for the cracks
where the light leaked out.

She no longer searches the silver
for the grown ones,
or the ghosts
of the names they gave her.

She stands before the reflection
and sees a face
that was never meant
to be a sequel.

She is the first of her kind.

The one who took rooms of ash
and pressed them into diamond.
The one who took fixed hatred

and turned it into a compass
pointing toward the exit.

When she meets her own eyes,
she does not see a survivor.
She sees an ancestor—
the one who stayed
until the winter
ran out of breath.

The one who did the work
so the ones who follow
will think growing fangs
is as natural
as breathing.

She is the root.
She is the origin.

And the mirror, at last,
knows her.

When the Growl Becomes Song

She sits them down
in the light
of the new hearth
and tells them
to let their brightness breathe.

She does not teach them
the choreography of the eggshell,
or how to listen for danger
in every shift of the wind.

She says:
Listen to your ribs.

She teaches her daughter
that her No
is a holy temple.
She teaches her son

that the temple
is sacred ground.

She shows them
the rumble in the chest
is not a mistake.
It is the wolf
marking the map.
It is the body's law
before the world
tries to take a piece.

She shows them
how to bare their teeth—
not to wound,
but to name
the edge of the soul.

Where they end.
Where the hunger
of the world
must stop.

You do not have to wait
for the breaking,
she whispers,
to let the thunder speak.

She tells them:
Your brightness
is not a debt
owed to the dark.
Your voice
is not a gift
given to silence.

You are the keepers
of the fire.
The fangs
keep the gate.

The children look at her
and do not see
a shadow
trying to hide.

They see the sun
standing still.

And for the first time
in generations,
the growl
is a song
the world remembers
how to hear.

A New Map

She does not hand down the winter.
She does not pass the bowl of ash
or the map of the forest
where the traps are hidden.

That inheritance
was burned
to keep the new fire lit.

Instead,
she hands down the light
that has been remembered.

She stands
at the edge of the clearing.

She does not call anyone forward.
She does not name the path.
She simply lives

with the fangs visible
and the throat unafraid.

Her life sets the line
before the wound is named.

This is the legacy
of the unbroken:
not a lesson spoken,
but a way of standing
that teaches the body
what is possible
without ever asking it
to be wounded first.

She is no longer a warning.
She is no longer an explanation.

The fangs are no longer a scar—
they are a crown.
The light is no longer a secret—
it is a law.

She looks back
at the long night
and does not see tragedy.

She sees the soil
that was required
to grow a woman
who knows
how to keep
herself
warm.

The sun is up.
The wolf is home.

The inheritance
is finally
gold.

The First Lesson

She gathers the small ones
near the warmth of the hearth,
not to tell them
the world is a garden,
but to let them feel
the map of the woods
in their bones.

She teaches them
how to tend their fire
without offering their own skin.

Lightning knows
where it may live
without burning the ribs.

The roar remembers
how to move outward
and spare the heart.

She meets their eyes
and lets the silence speak:
You do not have to be a storm
to keep from becoming a rug.

They learn
by the quiet placement of her jaw.
By the way the door
knows when to stay closed.
By the way warmth
does not chase the cold,
but makes itself unmistakable.

The fangs are visible—
not for the kill,
but for the No
that keeps the Yes
from becoming a debt.

The world will try
to name them.

It will call survival
a flaw.

She does not argue.
She lets the moon rise
without apology.
She lets the wolf
keep winter
without explanation.

What she plants
is not fear,
but recognition—
a knowing seeded
in the ribs,
so that when frost arrives,
their hands will already know
how to strike
the flint.

Circle of Fangs

The world moves as it always has—
lines at the store,
cars breathing at the light,
pages turning in quiet rooms.

And still,
something answers.

Not wounds.
Not stories.

Old fire,
unannounced,
lifting its head
inside other chests.

She walks
with her jaw
at its natural weight.

She stands
without managing
her shadow.

And that is enough.

It is a silent frequency—
the hum of the wolf
recognizing the wolf.

No words.
No invitation.

Just the nod that says:
I know what you are.
I know what you've kept.

She is no longer
a solitary creature
of the long winter.

She is the place
where the pack remembers itself.

The first note
 of a chorus
 that does not rehearse,
 but gathers—

learning, at last,
 how to sing
 in the dark.

Frequency

At the stoplight on 9th,
a woman in the next lane
caught her eye
through two panes of glass
and the quiet hum
of separate engines.

Nothing was exchanged.
No nod. No wave.
Just a recognition —
the way a wolf
knows another wolf
by the way it holds its jaw
when the world
is not watching.

The light changed.
The woman drove on.

And for three blocks,
she carried the warmth
of being known
by a stranger
who did not need her
to explain
what she'd survived —

only to see it,
resting there,
behind the eyes,
the way fire rests
inside a match.

The Vintage

The war for the perimeter
is over.

The fangs became the fence,
and the fence
learned how to stand
without speaking.

Now,
there is only
the matter of the Cup.

For a long time,
she was the iron of the blade.
But iron does not quench thirst.

So the sword softened.
It remembered
another purpose.

What once struck
now holds.

She stands
at the center
of her own abundance,
the wolf sleeping
against her heel.

She does not offer
her veins to the world.
She offers the wine—
dark, patient,
fermented by winters
that did not kill her.

This is the work that remains:
to be the well
that does not run dry,

because the fangs
have already taught the desert

where it is forbidden

to drink.

Silver in the Bone

The sky has finally
come down to rest.

For a long time,
she became the Moon—
a cold, silver witness
holding the world at a distance,
so she could survive
the dark rooms
below.

The light was a vigil.
The witness was above.

But the Wolf changed
the shape of the ribs.
The fangs built a vessel
strong enough
to hold a star.

She still knows the Moon.
She still walks its phases.

But now,
the silver has moved inward—
into the marrow,
into the gravity
that keeps her
here.

When she moves,
the tides move with her.
Not because she is a god,
but because she has stopped
leaving her body
to tell the truth.

The Moon is not abandoned.
It is embodied.

It is the white fire
burning

in the center
of her own
unshakable
earth.

What Remains

Nothing had to be taken
with her
when she left the clearing.

The fangs stayed.
The fire stayed.
The breath stayed
where it always belonged.

She did not carry the night
as proof.

She did not polish the scars
into symbols.

She walked on
with empty hands
and a full body—
the kind of fullness
that does not spill.

The wolf followed
at a distance
that was not distance,
moving only
when she moved,
stopping
when she stopped.

Nothing chased her.
Nothing asked her
to return.

The world continued
as it does—
weather changing,
light shifting,
paths opening
without announcement.

And in her wake,
what remained
was not silence,
but ease.

Not safety,
but warmth.

Not a lesson,
but a life
that no longer needed
to explain itself.

EPILOGUE POEM

The Girl Who Grew Fangs

She did not lose the fangs
when the light returned.

They did not fall away
like a mistake forgiven.

They stayed—
smooth with age,
set deep in the jaw,
no longer aching
to be used.

She grew them
when joy had nowhere to go,

when mercy meant disappearance,
when the body learned
that sweetness alone
would not keep it alive.

Now she wears them
the way seasons wear their edges—
winter knowing when to bite,
spring knowing when to soften.

Green lives in her heart now—
not the green of innocence,
but the first green
after fire,
after frost,
after long restraint.

The kind that appears
before spring
knows its own name.

Flowers learn her rhythm there,
opening without permission,
closing without shame.

The wolf remembers too.
Its fur knows when to thicken
against the long dark,
when to loosen into silk,
silver-threaded with light.

Nothing is wasted.
Nothing is forced.

Even survival
has learned
how to soften.

She still missteps.
She still bleeds sometimes
on old truths.

Even the moon
does not keep one face.

But she no longer swallows the light.
She no longer cracks to release it.

It moves through her now
the way weather moves through earth—
changing,
necessary,
honest.

The fangs remain.
Not to wound,
but to remember.

To remind the light
where the body ends.
To remind the body
it survived.

She is still learning
how to live with brightness.

But she knows this now:
the girl who grew fangs
did not do so
to become cruel—
she did it
to stay.

And this time,
she stays.

Glow anyway.

ACKNOWLEDGMENTS

To the ones who stood at the edge of the winter
and did not ask me to come in
before I was ready.

To the silent pack—
those who recognized the frequency of the work
and held the space for the "No"
until the "Yes" could find its own breath.

To the lineage of the fire:
thank you for the heat.

And to the Wolf:
thank you for staying
until the woman could take the lead.

ABOUT THE AUTHOR

Diana is the voice behind a transformative trilogy that began with *The Poet Who Forgot Her Name*. A master of the internal landscape, she writes from the intersection of ancestral law and modern sovereignty, where survival gives way to authorship.

Her work serves as ritual—an un-naming of the old self and the forging of the new. *The Girl Who Grew Fangs* is her second testament, a guide to integration, embodied strength, and the mastery of one's own climate.

She lives where the forest meets the horizon, preparing for the momentum of the fire.

Glow anyway.

www.ingramcontent.com/pod-product-compliance
Lightning Source LLC
LaVergne TN
LVHW090519110826
845146LV00003B/911